MAY 1 4 2008

GROWING
HOUSE PLANTS

Tracy Nelson Maurer

GREEN THUMB GUIDES

The Rourke Book Company, Inc.
Vero Beach, Florida 32964

Tracy Nelson Maurer specializes in nonfiction and business writing. Her most recently published children's books include the Bodyworks series, also from Rourke Publishing. A graduate of the University of Minnesota Journalism School, Tracy lives with her husband Mike and two children in Superior, Wisconsin.

With appreciation to gardeners Lois M. Nelson, Harvey Almstedt, and Lois I. Nelson; Sondra Landgreen and Brenda Moon, Bows and Boards Floral and Gifts; and Richard J. Zondag, Jung Seed Company.

PHOTO CREDITS:
All photos and illustrations © East Coast Studios

PRODUCED & DESIGNED by East Coast Studios
eastcoaststudios.com

EDITORIAL SERVICES:
Lois M. Nelson
Pamela Schroeder

Library of Congress Cataloging-in-Publication Data

Maurer, Tracy, 1965-
    Growing house plants / Tracy Nelson Maurer.
        p. cm. — (Green thumb guides)
    Includes bibliographical references (p.).
    Summary: Describes how to choose, plant, and care for various kinds of house plants.
    ISBN 1-55916-254-6
    1. Indoor gardening—Juvenile literature. 2. House plants—Juvenile literature. [1. Indoor gardening.
2. Gardening.] I. Title.

SB419.2 .M38 2000
635.9'65—dc21

                                                            00–026924

Printed in the USA

Table of Contents

Pet Plants

House plants can't play games or give you wet kisses like a puppy. However, house plants do one amazing trick. They help change the old air you breathe out into fresh air again. They make good "pets" for your home.

Any plant that grows indoors is a house plant, even if it started outdoors. They bring people and nature together. Bright blossoms and fruit grow on some plants. That makes indoor gardening exciting.

Fun Fact

House plants have flown with NASA scientists to work in space. They cleaned the old air in Skylab for the scientists.

House plants add color, smells, and shape to rooms everywhere.

Easy Plants to Grow

Indoor gardeners choose plants for the **foliage** (FO lee ij), or leaves. Foliage plants usually do not blossom, or grow flowers.

Some house plants will blossom. The African violet, Christmas cactus, and Easter lily grow cheery flowers. Many outdoor plants will also blossom inside. **Geraniums** (ji RAY nee umz) love to come indoors for the winter!

Gardeners choose foliage plants for the shape, color, and size of the leaves.

House plants come in all shapes and sizes. You can even grow lawn grass—your cat will love it!

To start gardening indoors, buy house plants from a **florist** (FLOHR ist) or **nursery** (NUR sur ee). An expert can warn you about harmful plants. The **philodendron** (fill oh DEN dron) grows easily but can poison small children.

Fun Fact

Holiday poinsettias look like big red, white, or pink flowers. Surprise! They are foliage plants. The bright colors come from the leaves.

Home Sweet Home

House plants make their homes in pots. Nearly anything that holds water will work. Try milk cartons, toy dump trucks, or even old shoes as "pots." Put a cookie sheet or waterproof tray under the pot to catch drips.

Some gardeners think clay pots work best. Leave the clay in water overnight before adding soil. Dry clay soaks water from the soil and keeps it from your plant. Put the clay pots inside pretty baskets or paint them different colors.

Plant a Garden Salad!

Small types of lettuce, carrots, and tomatoes will grow indoors. Use deep pots and put the plants in plenty of sunshine.

Soak new clay pots in water before you use them. This helps keep the soil from drying too fast.

Super Soil

Soil brings water, air, and food to your plant. Buy potting soil for indoor plants. Many stores, garden centers, and supermarkets sell potting soil. Don't use outdoor soil. Bugs make their homes there. You could bring them indoors. Yuck!

Indoor plants eat the **nutrients** (NEW tree ents) in potting soil. Feed your plants **fertilizers** (FUR tuh LIE zuhrz) in the spring and summer. Fertilizers put nutrients back in the soil. House plants use less water and food in the winter. Check with a florist to find the right food for your house plants.

Earthworm Neighbors

Let earthworms move in with your house plants. Bury a spoonful of kitchen scraps in the soil each week to feed them. They will reward you with healthy soil!

Put gardening charcoal (top) in the bottom of a pot to keep soil fresh. Vermiculite (middle) can be used alone or with soil for growing seeds. Potting soil (bottom) from a store comes mixed and ready for your pots.

Potting Your Plants

Give your plant a good home. Put a layer of clean stones in your pot. Add about two inches of potting soil. Place the roots on this soil. Try to keep sunlight from shining on the roots. The bottom leaves should stand about an inch over the top of the pot.

Put soil on top of a layer of stones. Planting is a fun way to get your hands dirty!

Your pot should have holes in the bottom to let water out. A layer of stones inside the pot keeps the soil from falling out.

Fill the pot with soil. Stop about an inch from the top. Pat the soil gently. Water your plant right away.

Fun Fact
Roots in the pot's drain holes mean the plant is "root bound." It needs more room to grow. Move it into a pot that is an inch bigger around.

Indoor Gardening Tools

Indoor gardeners need few tools. Your fingers do most of the work! Old forks and spoons work like little rakes and shovels. Use a cup for a watering can.

Many house plants enjoy a shower. Fill a clean spray bottle with water and mist the leaves. You may need to raise your green friend up into a sunny window. Try an upside-down flowerpot as a stand.

Use a drip-catcher under your pot. Coasters, cookie sheets, or dinner plates help keep water off windowsills or tabletops.

Tool Checklist

[ ] Old forks or spoons
[ ] Cup
[ ] Clean spray bottle
[ ] Flowerpot
[ ] Drip-catcher

Indoor gardeners use many things from around the house as tools.

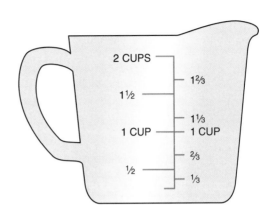

2 CUPS

1½

1 CUP

½

1⅔

1⅓

1 CUP

⅔

⅓

Perfect Places

Most house plants like to be just as warm as you do. Some **tropical** (TROP ih kuhl) plants may need a special place to grow. For example, **orchids** (OR kidz) need very hot, humid air.

If you feel cold, your plant also feels cold. Watch out for drafty doors and windows. Don't put your plant near heat vents or oven doors.

Every house plant likes some sunshine. A few like very sunny, hot windows. Others like shady corners. Check with a florist to learn the perfect place for your house plant.

Some house plants like to move outside for the summer. This plant likes a lot of sunshine. Not all plants do.

Water Me!

House plants need water to live. Some need a lot. Some need a little. Stick your finger into the soil about an inch deep. Wiggle it a bit. If the soil feels damp and looks like dark chocolate cake, your plant can wait for a drink. If the soil looks light, cracked, or crumbly, it's time to water.

STRING

IN WARM (NOT HOT!) WATER   BURY IN SOIL ABOUT 3" DEEP

A self-watering system works well if you plan to go away for more than a week.

Check the soil with your finger every three days. Does the soil feel crumbly? Your plant may need water.

Plants like to drink water that is a little warm. Water your plant until a little waters runs through the drain holes. Too much water drowns the roots. Empty the drip-catcher after you water.

Make a Self-Watering System

Bury one end of a thick string near the roots. Put the other end of the string in a bucket of water. The string carries the water to the soil when the plant needs it.

More and More Plants

Happy house plants grow fast. Soon your plants may need a trim or they will take over your room!

Save the leaves and stems you cut. Put them into a jar of water. In a few weeks, small white roots will grow underwater. When these roots are about two inches long, plant your "baby" plant in soil.

Plants that trail, or hang down from the pot, usually grow roots well in water. This is a fun way to share plants with other indoor gardeners.

A spider plant like this one sends out "baby" plants on long stems. You can cut the stems and plant the baby.

GLOSSARY

fertilizers (FUR tuh LIE zurz) — food for plants that gardeners add to the soil

florist (FLOHR ist) — a person who sells flowers or plants

foliage (FO lee ij) — the leaves of the plant

geraniums (ji RAY nee umz) — plants grown for their pretty red, pink, purple, or white flowers

nursery (NUR sur ee) — a place where plants are grown and sold

nutrients (NEW tree ents) — food for energy to grow

orchids (OR kidz) — tropical plants with fancy flowers

philodendron (fill oh DEN dron) — a plant that is easy to grow in sunny or shady rooms

tropical (TROP ih kuhl) — hot, humid weather; tropical plants like this kind of weather

House plants can grow for many years. Some get very big, like this bamboo palm.

INDEX

FURTHER READING

Find out more about gardening with these helpful books:

• Ambler, Wayne et al. *Treasury of Gardening.* Lincolnwood, Ill.: Publications International, 1994.

• Hart, Avery, and Paul Mantell. *Kids Garden!: The Anytime, Anyplace Guide To Sowing & Growing Fun.* Charlotte, Vermont: Williamson Publishing Co., 1996.

• *Rodale's Illustrated Encyclopedia of Gardening and Landscaping Techniques.* Edited by Barbara W. Ellis. Emmaus, Penn.: Rodale Press, 1990.

On-line resources:

Search for "kids gardening" on the World Wide Web to see many different sites.

• www.garden.org (c) National Gardening Association, 1999.